The City

Martin Crimp was born in 1956. His plays include *Definitely the Bahamas* (1987), *Dealing with Clair* (1988), *Play with Repeats* (1989), *No One Sees the Video* (1990), *Getting Attention* (1991), *The Treatment* (winner of the 1993 John Whiting Award), *Attempts on Her Life* (1997), *The Country* (2000), *Face to the Wall* (2002), *Cruel and Tender* (2004) and *Fewer Emergencies* (2005). A short fiction, *Stage Kiss,* was published in 1991 and *Four Imaginary Characters* appeared in 2000 as a preface to *Plays One,* followed in 2004 by *Four Unwelcome Thoughts.* He has a longstanding relationship with London's Royal Court Theatre, and more recently with the Vienna Festival and the Festival d'Automne in Paris, which commissioned his first text for music, *Into the Little Hill* (2006), written for composer George Benjamin. He has also translated works by Ionesco, Koltès, Genet, Marivaux, Molière and Chekhov.

MARTIN CRIMP

The City

faber and faber

First published in 2008
by Faber and Faber Limited
Bloomsbury House
74–77 Great Russell Street
London WC1B 3DA

Typeset by Country Setting, Kingsdown, Kent CT14 8ES
Printed and bound by CPI Group (UK) Ltd, Croydon, CR0 4YY

A CIP record for this book
is available from the British Library

ISBN 978–0–571–24011–1

6 8 10 9 7

Characters

Clair
Christopher
both heading for forty

Jenny
heading for thirty

Girl
a small girl of what? nine or ten?

Time
Blank

Place
Blank

THE CITY

*Everything we do, in art and life,
is the imperfect copy of what we intended*

Fernando Pessoa
The Book of Disquiet

I

Clair holds a flat object in a plain paper bag.

After a while Chris comes on. He's wearing a suit, carries a case, has a security pass hanging from his neck.

Chris How was your day?

Clair My day was fine. Only—

Chris Oh?

Clair Only—yes—I was waiting on the station concourse this afternoon after my meeting—waiting for my train— when this man came up to me and said, have you seen a little girl about so high—I've lost her.

Chris Lost her?

Clair Well that's what I said. I said what d'you mean lost her?—what does she look like? He said, I've told you: she's about so high and she's wearing pink jeans. I said well in that case I've just seen her—she was heading for the taxi rank with a woman who looked like a nurse— I can't say for certain she was a nurse, but it looked as if she had a uniform on, under her coat. So then he says, why didn't you stop them?

Chris It wasn't your responsibility to stop them.

Clair Exactly. But of course that's not what I said—what I said to him was: well let's call the police. And that's when it turned out no no no it was nothing as serious as he'd led me to believe. Because the girl was his daughter, and the woman—who—I was right—is a nurse at a

7

nearby hospital—the Middlesex—was his sister-in-law. The girl—because they'd just got off the train—the girl had been brought here to stay with the sister-in-law. But the man—the father—had decided at the last moment to buy his little girl a diary. So he'd gone into a shop to buy his little girl a diary. But when he came out with the diary, expecting his kiss, they'd gone.

Chris His kiss.

Clair Yes, to be kissed goodbye. I mean by his little girl. He said he didn't expect to be kissed goodbye by his sister-in-law because his sister-in-law despised him. Which is why—thinking about it—not me, I mean him, him thinking about it—maybe why the moment he was out of sight she'd deliberately dragged the little girl off.

Chris What? Was she being dragged?

Clair No—but they were moving quite fast. Maybe not fast for the nurse, but fast for the little girl.

Chris That's why you noticed the jeans.

Clair That's right.

Chris Because her legs were having to move quickly you mean to keep up with this woman, this nurse, this aunt dragging her to the taxi rank.

Clair Well no—I've said—not dragging—but yes—I certainly did notice the jeans.

Pause.

What about you?

Chris Mmm?

Clair How was your day?

Chris My day was good. Only my card wouldn't swipe. Took me fifteen minutes to get into my own building.

Clair Oh no. Why was that?

Chris Well I tapped on the glass and the only person in there was a cleaner so the cleaner came over to the glass and I held up my card and pointed, obviously, at my picture on the card, but the cleaner just shrugged—which is odd because I know all those cleaners really well.

Clair So what did you do?

Chris Buzzed the buzzer till somebody came. (*Slight pause.*) What's that?

Clair What's wrong?

Chris Wrong? Nothing. Why?

Clair It's just the way you said: 'What's that?'

Chris Nothing's wrong.

Clair Good.

Chris Nothing's wrong.

Clair Good. I'm pleased nothing's wrong. Because I wanted to show you this.

Chris What's that? The diary?

Clair He gave me the diary—yes. I said: you mustn't give me this—it's for your daughter. Because of course the idea had been for his little girl to write down all her thoughts and feelings about this big change in her life.

Chris What big change in her life?

Clair Leaving her father of course. Living with her aunt.

Pause.

Have you not been / listening?

Chris Does it start in January?

Clair What?

Chris Does it start in January?

Clair Yes—it's just a normal diary.

Chris What're you going to do with it?

Clair I don't know.

Chris Write in it?

Clair I don't know.

Chris Write what?

Clair I've told you: I have / no idea.

Chris And he just *gave* it to you?

Clair Mmm?

Chris The man—this man—he just *gave* it to you?

Clair Well no—not right there—obviously—in the middle of Waterloo Station. He asked if he could talk to me. So because of what had happened—the little girl and so on—the fact I'd seen her heading off like that towards the taxis—I felt I didn't really have a choice. And I was glad, as it happened, because it turned out I knew him.

Chris You knew him?

Clair Yes—not knew him—but knew who he was.

Chris Oh?

Clair Yes. Well yes. He's this writer that everyone's talking about. Well not everyone—obviously—but people who know—people who know about writing. So of course that was completely fascinating—it was completely fascinating to find myself sitting in a café with this writer that everyone's talking about. Because he never gives interviews, but there he was sitting in this café opening his heart to me. About his time in prison—and the torture there—but all quite normally—just a normal conversation—just like me talking to you now—about torture—about the bucket on the cement floor—all quite normal—and the child of course—his little girl—the hopes he had for her—which made him sad—why is it, he said to me, that it's our hopes that make us sad—even there—in the dark—in the cell—which is why he tried not to—hope, I mean—I think I've got this right—during all the nights and days he waited for them to come—just waited and waited for them to come.

Chris Them?

Clair His torturers.

Chris I see.

Clair The people who were determined to / break his will.

Chris I had a visit from Bobby today.

Pause.

Clair Oh? Bobby Williams?

Chris Yes.

Clair What did Bobby Williams want?

Chris Just to say hello. Well—no—more in fact than to say hello. He came into my office because he wanted to tell me about this lunch he'd had with Jeanette. Because the week before last it seems he'd had this lunch with Jeanette and according to Jeanette the North American division is beginning to restructure and Jeanette's instinct is, is that if they're beginning to restructure in North America it won't be long before they start restructuring here.

Clair Oh?

Chris And of course he managed to make all this sound as if he cares about what happens to me and to my family but the truth is he wanted to see me squirm. And because of his relationship with Jeanette—which I would hesitate to call sexual—but because of this thing, whatever it is, this intimacy, these lunches they have—well because of that, Bobby's job is protected, whereas mine, given the situation in the North American territories, is, well is obviously much more vulnerable.

Clair Look: if the changes are going to be that radical, then even Jeanette won't be able to protect Bobby for the simple reason that Jeanette will be vulnerable herself.

Chris Yes, but Jeanette's very clever. I'm not saying she's indispensable—nobody's indispensable—but she's worked out a way of printing herself onto people's minds. I mean let's say, let's just say that this afternoon, instead of meeting this man at Waterloo Station, you'd met Jeanette, and that it was Jeanette who'd taken you to a café and told you this ridiculous story about the little girl and the nurse and about being tortured in a bucket or whatever it is this man tried to make you believe. Well in those two hours in the café—because I'm assuming you spent a good couple of hours with him—but in those two hours Jeanette would have made it her business to print herself onto your mind. You'd come away from that café, and regardless of her ridiculous story, or perhaps, who knows, because of it, you'd be thinking that Jeanette—and I've seen this happen—was essential to your company's survival. You'd be talking to me now—having, as you say, a normal conversation with me now—but in your head there'd be this current—this flow of speculation about Jeanette—Jeanette's grasp of the market—Jeanette's strategic vision—Jeanette's ability to think outside of the box blah blah blah. And once that flow started there would be no way you could ever dismiss her from your thoughts—the way for example you'll almost certainly dismiss this man.

Clair Oh?

Chris Yes.

Clair A flow of speculation.

Chris Yes. And you'd have no idea why. Because after all Jeanette is very ordinary-looking.

Clair Is she?

Chris And yet she has this power.

Clair Over men.

Chris Over what?—no—that's not at all what I mean— I mean over everyone—men and women / likewise.

Clair So you're saying you may lose your job?

Chris I'm just saying what Bobby told me Jeanette said to him at lunch. It doesn't mean I'm going to kill myself. I have no plans to hang myself from a tree, if that's what you think. There are, as you are well aware, two small children sleeping in this house, and I'm not going to leave them fatherless, any more than I'm prepared to let my decomposing body be found by someone out walking their dog. I hardly think I'm unemployable. And even someone who's spent a whole meeting with their head down drawing interlocking shapes on the agenda—or imaginary animals—will often come up to me afterwards and thank me for being the only person in the room to 've talked sense. Even Bobby Williams would grant me that. So I really don't think you need to be afraid.

Clair Afraid of what?

Chris Because obviously this kind of rumour is unsettling.

Clair I'm not afraid.

Chris Then why are you smiling?

Clair Am I?

Chris You know you're smiling.

Clair I had no idea I was smiling. (*Slight pause.*) Am I still smiling?

Chris You know you are.

Clair Then I must be smiling in spite of myself. Or perhaps I'm smiling because I'm looking at you in that suit of yours and remembering how much I love you. But—well—listen—what makes you think I've dismissed him from my thoughts?

Chris I'm sorry?

Clair Why do you call his story ridiculous? What makes you think I've dismissed Mohamed from my thoughts?

Chris Dismissed who?

Clair The writer. Mohamed. What makes you think I've dismissed him from my thoughts?

Chris Well haven't you?

Clair Yes—no—no—not necessarily.

Pause.

He begins to laugh.

What is it?

Chris You've stopped smiling.

Clair Have I?

Chris Yes.

Clair Really?

Chris Yes.

They both chuckle.

I'll tell you something that will make you laugh. You know this morning when I got to my building? Well my card wouldn't swipe. I tried and I tried but it *would not swipe*. So I tapped on the glass but the only person in there at that time of the morning was a cleaner so the cleaner came over to the glass . . . No. I've told you this. Have I already told you this?

Clair Go on.

Chris But I've already told you this.

Clair Told me what? Have you?

Chris About the cleaner coming over to the glass. About when I held up my card.

Clair Oh *that*.

Chris Well didn't I?

Clair Yes.

Chris So why did you say go on? (*Slight pause.*) Hmm.

Clair What is it?

Chris Nothing. Nothing at all. Where're you going?

Clair I'm going to put this somewhere safe.

Clair goes out with the diary. Chris remains. He does nothing.

II

Clair works at a computer, referring to a book or manuscript beside her.

Chris appears—'casually' dressed.

He stands behind her, watching her work. She takes no notice. Time passes, then:

Chris Don't you get bored with it?

Clair Mmm?

Chris Translating. Don't you get / bored with it?

Clair (*continuing to work*) Well of course I get bored with it sometimes. Not everything people write is interesting and even interesting writing—like this—can be dull to translate. On the other hand, I do get to meet authors, and some of them are real characters—they take me out to dinner—introduce me to their families. Some of them are much quieter. They're the crabs. As soon as you pick up the stone they're hiding under, they scuttle off to another one. D'you have to keep standing behind me like that?

He doesn't move. She continues to work.

Chris So you're not ever tempted.

Clair Tempted to do what?

Chris To write something of your own.

Clair Me? (*Smiles, and turns to him for the first time.*) What makes you say that?

He starts to walk away.

What makes you say that? Where are you going?

Chris It was the doorbell.

Clair What doorbell? I didn't hear it. Are you sure?

Chris I'm pretty sure I heard the doorbell.

He goes off.

She listens out for a moment and, hearing nothing, continues to work.

Finally he returns with a woman, Jenny, who is wearing a nurse's uniform under her coat. They are talking as they appear.

Chris Please. I'm sure you won't be disturbing her. She's just here—look—in the garden—working.

Jenny I don't want to disturb anyone.

Chris I really don't think she minds—do you?

Clair Minds what?

Chris This is—sorry.

Jenny Jenny.

Chris This is Jenny.

Jenny I'm Jenny. Hello.

Chris Can I get you something, Jenny—something to drink.

Jenny Oh no. I can't stop. (*To Clair.*) I just wondered if we could talk for a moment.

Clair I'd be very happy to. Let me just take these things back inside.

Chris I'll do that if you like.

Clair No. You stay here and talk to Jenny.

She gathers up her things and goes. Pause.

Chris So . . . you're a nurse.

Jenny Yes.

Chris Have you always been a nurse?

Jenny Yes.

Pause.

Chris I suppose a lot of nurses are men.

Jenny A lot of nurses—you're right—are men. But a surprising number of nurses—perhaps the majority of nurses in fact—are women.

Chris Is that so.

Jenny Oh yes.

Chris But you must be under a great deal of pressure.

Jenny We are all of us—yes—men and women—under an intense pressure. (*Pause.*) And sometimes the pressure is *so* intense . . . it's *so* intense that . . . (*She laughs.*) But this is such a beautiful garden. I can see it from my window. I often see your children running up and down shouting and screaming. I often think how extraordinary it is to see a garden like yours with children running up and down shouting and screaming—right here—right here in the middle of a city.

Chris Isn't our garden just like all the other gardens? Surely the city's full of this kind of garden—a patch of grass—a few plants round the edge we typically don't know the names of. I don't really understand what you're saying.

18

Jenny Of course there are similar gardens—but now I'm in your garden—right inside your garden—actually standing here—actually standing on this patch of grass— I realise that your garden genuinely is unique. We know each other, don't we. I've seen you somewhere—was it the opticians? Or I know what it is—looking in a freezer cabinet in the supermarket—digging right down into the packs of frozen vegetables—looking at the broccoli— digging right down—that was you—only you were wearing a suit—you must've been coming home from work.

Chris Yes.

Jenny Picking up some shopping on the way home from work.

Chris Yes.

Jenny And also—

Chris You're right.

Jenny I'm sure I've seen you—

Chris Oh?

Jenny Yes—standing at an upstairs window.

Chris You're right.

Jenny Because when you opened the door I thought to myself: I've seen that face before—in the supermarket or something—or standing at an upstairs window looking a bit sad.

Chris Can I take your coat?

Jenny What?

Chris Your coat.

Jenny Oh no. I can't stay. I'm working. (*Slight pause.*)
I did want to talk to your wife, though.

Chris I'll call her.

Jenny No—please don't raise your voice. It frightens me.

Chris Well in that case I'll go and find her.

*He goes. Jenny waits. She takes out a mirror and
examines her face. The other two come back and
watch her in silence. Then:*

Clair You wanted to talk to me?

Jenny Yes.

Clair What about?

Jenny Mmm?

Clair What about?

Jenny You sound surprised that I want to talk to you,
but the fact is we're neighbours, and even if your house
is much bigger than my tiny flat, we still—or at least
I imagine we do—still care about the same things: street
lighting, one-way systems, noise levels and so on. Not
only that, but we're both women—which means—well
I hope it does—that unlike men we can hopefully define
our territory without having to piss on it first.

Clair Do I know you?

Jenny I'm Jenny. I've told you who I am. We're
neighbours. You've probably seen me getting into my
car—or—like your husband over there—watched me in
the mornings taking off my uniform when I've driven
back totally exhausted from the hospital at a time when
most people are getting up and listening to the radio
while they have their breakfast. In fact I could probably
fall asleep there and then, but what I like to do instead is

curl up in a chair with a nice piece of toast or a nice egg
and watch one of those old black-and-white films on TV.
Today for example there was the one where Humphrey
Bogart pretends to be in love with Audrey Hepburn but
ends up really loving her—really and truly loving her.
After that—well you've probably heard—I like to play
the piano for a bit. I'm not too bad at playing the
piano—I took it quite seriously as a child—and I always
warm up with scales and things like that—but the funny
thing is, is that although I can get all the notes and
understand just how intensely the composer must've
imagined it, there's no life to my playing. Emotionally
it's dead. Because you know what it's like when the sun
shines on the TV screen so the picture disappears and
all you see is the glass surface of it? Well that's what my
playing's like—hard and colourless. I'm not saying that
if you heard me in the street on a summer's day when
I had the windows open you wouldn't think 'Oh—
exquisite.' But if you stopped and began to listen—began
to really really listen—then the expression on your face
would turn—oh yes—believe me—to dread—the same
look I see on a patient's face when they're told that the
tumour growing in their lungs has now spread to the
brain—a kind of hardening—here—round the eyes—
because of course once that point's been reached then
death—well I'm sure you both know this—is inevitable.
But listen: I didn't come here to talk about my piano
playing.

Clair Oh?

Jenny Of course not.

Chris Then why have you—?

Jenny Yes?

Chris Then why have you—?

Jenny Yes? Come? Why have I come?

Chris Exactly.

Clair To talk to me.

Chris Mmm?

Clair To talk to me.

Jenny That's right.

Chris I'll take your coat.

Jenny No. Keep away.

Chris I'm sorry?

Jenny I said: keep away from me.

She smiles. Slight pause. To Clair:

Let me explain. I work hard. I get tired. I'm finding it difficult to sleep. My husband's gone to war. Not to kill. Of course not. He's a doctor. He has a gun—because all soldiers have guns—but you'd laugh if you saw the tiny tiny gun they give to doctors—no use at all for killing people—not the large numbers of people you have to kill in a war. It's a secret war. I can't tell you where it is, or I'd be putting lives at risk. But I *can* tell you that what they're doing now, in the secret war, is they're attacking a city—pulverising it, in fact—yes—turning this city—the squares, the shops, the parks, the leisure centres and the schools—turning the whole thing into a fine grey dust. Because—and I have my husband's word for this—everybody in that city has to be killed. Not by him. Of course not. He's a doctor. But all the same the city has to be pulverised so that the boys—our boys—can safely go in and kill the people who are left—the people, I mean, still clinging on to life. (*Slight pause.*) Because it's amazing how people can cling on to life—I'm a nurse—I see it

22

every day—I see people cling on to life almost every day—and it's the same—according to my husband—in this city: people in all sorts of unexpected places, clinging on to life. So the boys—what the boys have to do is they have to go in and kill the people clinging on to life. And just to make things clear, they've got blue cards, and on the cards, that's what it says: kill. And I know what you're thinking: you're thinking it must be pretty easy to kill people who are simply clinging on to life—any fool could do that, you're thinking—it must be like—what?—going round your house before you go away on holiday—pulling the plugs out. But no—ah—well—no—because—you see—and I have my husband's word for this—the people clinging on to life are the most dangerous people of all. (*Slight pause.*) Say you're one of the boys—and you're patrolling a street and you notice an open hatch—and the hatch leads to a drain—so you go into the drain—you go into the drain because you think: hmm—perhaps there's life in this drain—perhaps there are people clinging on to life in this drain. And yes—listen—sounds—scratching—sucking sounds—signs of life in the dark—because it's pretty dark—of course it is—down there—deep under the city—in the drain. So you drop your goggles over your eyes and you can see—yes—actually see—according to my husband— in the dark—you can see the whole grey-green world of the drain using your goggles in the dark. (*Slight pause.*) And yes—look—here are the signs—here are the signs of people clinging on to life: rags, blood, coffee cups—and the stink of course—I'm a nurse—I smell it every day—the particular stink people make when they're clinging and clinging on to life. And there they are! 'Suddenly', like it says in a book, there they are: a bright green woman with a bright grey baby at her breast—right there at the end of the drain—sucking—that was the sound you heard—a woman giving suck. (*Slight pause.*) So the boy thinks: (*without characterising*) 'Hmm, fuck this, fuck this you bitch. I can't just—well—kill. I can't kill a woman with a baby at her breast you cunt, you fucking bitch. Hmm, I know what I'll do: I'll get out my blue card and I'll check the rules, I'll see what it says about this, about mothers and their babies, in the rules.' So he reaches for his blue card to check the rules and that's when they're on him. Angry fuckers clinging to life in the drain. Angry and unscrupulous perpetrators of terror who'll stop at nothing to stay alive—use a mother and her baby simply to stay alive. A brick splits the soldier's skull. And the last thing the baby sees as its mother uses her finger to slip its mouth off her nipple is a serrated kitchen knife— and I have my husband's word for this—a small knife with a stainless serrated blade being used to cut the soldier's heart out—d'you see? (*Slight pause.*) I said: d'you see?

Clair Well . . .

Jenny Do you?

Clair Yes—of course—well no—see what?

Chris See what exactly?

Jenny I'm not talking to you. Keep out of it.

Clair See what, Jenny?

Jenny How difficult it is to sleep.

Clair Oh?

Jenny How difficult it is—yes—for me to sleep in the daytime with all this on my mind when your children are running up and down shouting and screaming. D'you see?

Clair (*faint laugh*) What—d'you want me to lock them indoors?

Jenny Would you?

Clair What?

Jenny Would you lock them indoors?

Clair Of course not. Of course we wouldn't lock our children indoors. Would we?

Chris Of course not.

Jenny Where are they now then?

Chris They're playing. They're playing in the playroom.

Clair That's right: they're playing in the playroom.

Jenny Locked in?

Clair No.

Jenny Locked in the playroom?

Clair No.

Slight pause. Clair and Chris exchange a glance and chuckle. Softly:

What makes you think we lock our children in the playroom, Jenny? The playroom doesn't even have a key.

Chris It doesn't have a lock, let alone a key.

Clair I think it has a lock.

Chris Does it?

Clair I think it does—yes—have a lock. But the point is—Jenny—

Chris I'll go and look.

Clair What?

Chris You've made me curious. I'll go and look.

He goes. Slight pause.

Clair (*lowering voice*) I'm afraid he's got like this since he lost his job. He's bored and he's always looking for things to do. That's why he wanted to take your coat. To feel useful. And when he brought it back to you, he wouldn't't've just handed you the coat—oh no—he's started holding my coat up and expecting me to slip my arm gratefully into the sleeve, like some character out of those old films you talked about. (*Smiles.*) And of course being a man he makes them play these games—these horrible noisy games—makes them scream—shout out—shriek—tosses them into the air—pretends—I hate it—I can't watch—to drop them on their heads—when they'd rather—obviously—watch TV or a blackbird—well, wouldn't you?—building its nest. You're right, Jenny—we're women—we don't have to bang our fists on the table to make a point and the point you're making is a fair one. And the fact that summer's coming—obviously—makes it even worse. Because if you shut your windows, you won't be able to breathe, and if you open them—because I do understand this—even when the shouting and screaming stops—*if* it stops—instead of going to sleep, you'll lie there waiting and waiting for it to start again, even if it never does—a kind of torture, really. (*Smiles.*) I don't know what the solution is, Jenny. I can ask my husband—what—to cut his toenails—I can turn away my head if I don't want to be kissed (although of course that's more dangerous)—but what I can't do—Jenny—is ask him not to play with his own children—in the daytime—when he has no job—in his own garden.

Jenny What then?

Clair Mmm?

Jenny What can you do?

Clair There's nothing I can do. I'm very sorry.

Chris comes back, laughing.

Chris Incredible.

Clair What is?

Chris They *are* locked in.

Clair What d'you mean?

Chris You were right: there *is* a lock—they've locked themselves in—they've found a key.

Clair What key?

Chris Well they must've found one.

Clair What did you say to them?

Chris Well I told them to unlock the door immediately.

Jenny They've found a key?

Chris I can only think it was under the carpet. They must've pulled up the carpet and found a key—yes.

Jenny (*laughs*) Devils.

Chris Yes.

Clair What did you say to them?

Chris I've told you: I asked them to come out. I asked them what they thought they were playing at. I asked them if they realised just how dangerous it was to pull up a carpet and lock themselves in a room. Because now, I said to them, now, even if you get the door unlocked, there's no guarantee that you'll be able get the door open, because it will jam against the carpet. You'll be trapped, I said, you'll be trapped in that playroom, and if either of you has an accident in there—cuts yourself, for example, and starts losing blood—then how will Mummy and Daddy be able to help you?

Slight pause.

Clair What did they say?

Chris Nothing.

Clair You're sure they're in there?

Chris Well of course they're in there. The door's locked.

Jenny She means maybe they've locked the door from the outside then run away.

Chris I know exactly what she means—I don't need you to explain to me what she means—but the fact is, is I heard their voices and if they haven't unlocked that door in another— (*Looks at watch.*) what shall we say?—forty-five seconds?—

He concentrates on his watch. The two women look at him. Ten seconds of this.

III

Chris exactly as he was, concentrating on his watch.
After ten seconds, Clair appears, in a light summer dress.

Clair You look funny. What're you doing?

Chris Mmm? (*Looks up.*)

Clair What're you doing?

Chris Funny?

Clair Yes. What're you doing?

Chris (*smiles*) You've been on that phone for over an hour.

Clair Have I? Sorry. I've been talking to one of my writers. He's inviting me to Lisbon. In October. Did you want to use the phone then?

Chris October.

Clair Yes—well—I say one of my writers, but it's the same writer—the one I met at the train station—Mohamed?—remember?—he'd lost his child? Anyway he's organising a conference—a conference about translation—and he's asked me to give a paper.

Chris Mohamed.

Clair Yes—don't you remember—last Christmas—he'd lost his little girl.

Slight pause.

Chris Won't it be hot?

Clair I like the heat. You mean in Lisbon?

Chris Yes.

Clair I like the heat. You know that. (*Slight pause.*) Is something funny?

Chris No.

Clair Then what does that look mean?

Chris It simply means I suddenly realise how much I love you.

Clair Oh?

Chris Yes.

Clair You suddenly realise?

Chris Yes.

Clair Fuck off.

Chris What?

Clair I said: fuck off. You're only saying you love me because you feel bad about yourself and you hope that saying you love me will make you feel like a better person than you really are.

Chris On the contrary: I'm saying I love you because I feel good about myself. I have some very good news.

Clair Oh?

Chris Yes.

Clair Is it about work?

Chris Yes.

Clair You've found a job.

Chris Yes. (*Slight pause.*) I've found a job. Aren't you happy for me?

Clair I'm very happy for you. (*Slight pause.*) What's wrong?

Chris Kiss me.

Clair No.

Chris Hold my hand.

Clair No—why?—not now. (*Slight pause.*) It's hot. (*Slight pause, smiles.*) Well anyway how did this happen?

Chris Won't you kiss me?

Clair Not now. Not when it's hot.

Chris I thought you liked the heat.

Clair What? I do like the heat. Of course I like the heat. But not being kissed in it, that's all.

Chris In which case I'm sorry.

Clair Don't apologise. Impose your will.

Chris What?

Clair Impose your will.

   Slight pause.

Chris You mean force you to kiss me?

Clair (*laughs*) How could you force me to kiss you?

Chris I could come over to you. I could force you.

Clair Oh?

Chris Yes.

Clair How will you do that?

Chris I'll show you. I'll come over to you. I'll make you. It's simple.

Clair Is it?

Chris It's really very simple: I'll come over to you and I'll force you to kiss me.

Clair Go on then.

Chris If that's what you want.

Clair Go on then.

Chris Is that what you want?

Clair Why should I want that? What kind of woman would want that?

He doesn't move.

Jeanette?

Chris Who?

Clair Jeanette?

Slight pause.

Chris Is that what you want?

Clair It's no good asking me what I want, you have to impose your will. You have to impose your will or you'll be (*snaps fingers*) out, you'll be (*snaps fingers*) out of that plate-glass door before you've even arranged our photos on your desk. Because the world has changed— oh yes—and you'll have to be much stronger than this.

Chris I *am* much stronger than this.

Clair Then prove it.

A slight pause. He goes over to her. He touches her face, touches her hair. She doesn't react but she doesn't resist. At the last moment he goes to kiss her, but she twists her head violently away.

No! (*Smiles.*) And anyway how did this happen, how did all of this happen? How did you come to get this job or whatever it is—mmm?

Chris It's quite a long story, as a matter of fact. And I can't remember if I told you what happened at the end of last year but at the end of last year when the restructuring began, Jeanette got herself voted onto the board and the first thing she did in her new capacity as executive member was to quite unexpectedly force Bobby Williams—I think I told you this—to resign. And early in the New Year perhaps I didn't mention that Bobby was found dead in a hotel room in Paris where he'd told his family he was going for a job interview.

Well soon after the funeral in—hmm, when was that?— March?—I'd gone down to the supermarket one evening to buy meat and because I couldn't find the quantity of meat I wanted in the pre-packed section—I mean in the plastic boxes where they put the meat on the little absorbent mats—I had to go to the meat counter and there was something very familiar about the man behind the meat counter and it turned out we'd been at school together. I know—yes—incredible. I didn't know who *he* was, but he recognised me straight away, he said, 'I can see you don't remember me, but I know who *you* are, I recognised you straight away, you're Christopher, we went to the same school, it's the hat.' I said, 'How d'you mean—the hat?' He said, 'No one recognises me in this hat.' So he took off the hat—one of those white muslin trilby things they make them wear in the supermarket and I concentrated on his eyes and I realised there was in fact something really familiar about this person's eyes. So I said to him, 'Yes, you're right, I do remember you, but I'm sorry, even without the hat I don't remember your name.' So he goes, 'You don't have to remember it: my name's right here.' And what he meant of course was he

33

was wearing a name badge and on the badge was 'Sam'. Of course. Sam. Sam from school. Jesus Christ. So I asked him how things were going—how life was treating him—which was really stupid because I could see that life was treating him like shit: wearing a badge, dressed in a stupid hat—but no—oh no—life was treating him well, he said—the pay and conditions were well above average—there was a friendly atmosphere and generous discounts for staff—job security—good prospects—he'd no complaints—what about myself? So I explained to him that I was . . . well . . . what's the word . . . (*Bows head.*) Hmm.

Slight pause. Lifts head.

He's changed into this navy-blue tracksuit and we're sitting in this pub and he buys me a drink and he says, 'You probably don't remember the day you spat on me—spat all over my clothes—spat all over my face—cornered me in the classroom with that friend of yours and spat on me. You probably don't remember that, Christopher. You probably don't remember spitting on my hair. Cheers.' (*Bows head.*)

Slight pause. Head still bowed.

We're sitting in the pub, we've had a few drinks, there's me, there's Sam, and now there's Sam's friend Phil who works in the warehouse, drives a fork-lift. Who's your friend, says Phil. This, says Sam, is my old friend Christopher from school, done very well for himself, lost his job, arsehole, scuse my French. Oh, says Phil, sorry to hear it mate, seen Indy? Not here yet? Maybe it's the flight, says Sam, maybe there's fog, where's she coming from? Abu Dhabi, says Phil, fucked if there's fog there, what's she playing at? Give her a chance, says Sam, beautiful girl like that.

34

Slight pause. Lifts head.

Okay—listen—I'm on my own—I'm in the pub—I've
had a few drinks—Indy walks in—I know it's her from
the logo on her jacket—the skirt—the works—the little
bag on wheels—Indy, I say to her, Phil's gone—I'm really
sorry but he wouldn't wait. Beg your pardon? says
Indy—who are you? where's Phil? what's going on? So
I try to explain—about the meat—about Sam from
school—his eyes—the white hat—treating him well—no
complaints—and she's looking at me—that's right— like
that—the way you're looking at me now—the same
disdain—this girl Indy—the same disdain—the way she
looks at the men in business class when they order
champagne—touch her arm and order champagne for
the girls they've left their wives for—silver-haired men
watching the river turn to threads—cities to maps—
whole oceans to a field of sparks—utter contempt—
yes—like that—like you—that look—BECAUSE WHAT
IS IT EXACTLY YOU'RE TRYING TO SAY TO ME?

Silence.

Clair Look. I'm just going to Lisbon for a few days.
It won't be till October. I don't despise you. Of course
I don't. And why should you care about the opinion of
a complete stranger in a pub? It's not as if you'll ever see
her again.

Chris No.

Clair Is it?

Chris No.

Clair Will you?

Chris No. (*Slight pause.*) Jesus Christ, no, I hope not.

Clair (*smiles*) Then stop thinking about it.

Chris I'm not thinking about it.

Clair Good—because you should stop thinking about it.

Chris Well I'm not.

Slight pause.

Clair I'm so happy for you.

Chris Oh?

Clair It's such wonderful news.

Chris Yes.

Clair You've changed completely.

Chris Yes. What? Have I?

Clair Yes, you've completely changed. You're much more . . .

Chris Am I?

Clair Of course you are.

Chris More what?

Clair More confident.

Chris Am I?

Clair Of course you are. Look at you.

Chris More confident.

Clair Yes. Look at you. Much more confident. You're a different man.

Slight pause: he bows his head.

Well don't you feel like a completely different man?

Chris Yes.

Clair Your whole attitude's changed.

Chris Yes.

Clair Even the way you're standing.

Chris Yes.

Pause. His head remains bowed.

Yes I suppose you're / right.

Clair Because let's face it: you've been impossible. You've stormed round this house shouting and slamming doors ever since Christmas. I close all the windows, but even then—well as you know, even then the neighbours turn up here complaining they can't sleep—and I can see them looking at the children, wondering if there are bruises under their dressing-up clothes. When I've tried to work you've sat at the other end of the table writing shopping lists, or stood behind me, criticising my choice of words. You've almost stopped being interested in sex—and when you have been interested, it's felt like a business opportunity, or a bank loan—forgive me—arranged over the phone. But now—

Chris Yes.

Clair But now—

Chris You're right.

Clair But now—

Chris Now what?

Clair Because I'd been dreading summer, but now your whole attitude's changed.

Chris Even the way I'm standing.

Clair Yes.

Chris Even the way the trees look. Even the roses have changed.

37

Clair Yes. Even the forget-me-nots.

Chris You know what we ought to do.

Clair What's that?

Chris We ought to celebrate. We ought to all get in the car and celebrate. We ought to all drive up the motorway into the oncoming traffic and celebrate. Don't you think? Or I know what: invite someone round.

Clair Who?

Chris People—people we know—friends. Bobby for example.

Clair What d'you mean: Bobby?

Chris Bobby—Bobby Williams—invite him round to celebrate—eh? Get him to bring Jeanette.

Slight pause.

Clair (*laughs*) I don't think that's funny.

Chris He's a friend. He's someone we know.

Clair (*laughs*) Stop it.

Chris Because there are a number of things, sweetheart, I don't quite understand—and some of them are things I'll never understand—and I'm quite happy for there to be some things I'll never understand—but one of the things I don't understand but that I really would like to understand is why you say that it's hot. Because—well— what with the trees and so on—what with the shade and the air—because I can feel it—moving through the house—see what I mean? (*Slight pause.*) You see what I mean about the heat? You see what I mean about not wanting to be kissed?

Clair (*laughs*) Who doesn't want to be kissed?

Chris You don't.

Clair (*laughs*) What makes you say that?

Chris Well do you?

Clair (*laughs*) What? Want to be kissed?

Chris Do you?

Clair It's no good *asking*.

Chris Mmm?

Clair It's no good *asking* me. (*Slight pause.*) It's no good asking a woman if she wants / to be kissed.

Chris Well shall I assume that you do, then? Shall I come over to you? Shall I assume—mmm?—that that's what you want? (*Slight pause.*) Listen: I'm going to assume that that's what you want.

Clair Go on then.

Chris I'm going—you're right—to impose my will.

Clair Go on then.

He doesn't move. Slight pause.

Chris Are you crying? Why are you crying? Don't cry. Why are you crying?

Clair BECAUSE I AM ANGRY.

On this line, music in the distance from Jenny's flat: Schubert, 'Moments Musicaux', No. 3 in F minor. Pause. The music plays.

Chris I don't understand. You were laughing. Just a moment ago you were laughing (*Slight pause.*) Bruises? Why did you say that? Why would anyone think we'd harm our children? We love our children—love's what brought them into the world. Well didn't it—didn't it?

39

Pause. Music continues.

You're being unreasonable.

Clair (*wiping her eyes*) Where're you going?

Chris I'm going to watch TV.

Clair I thought you wanted to celebrate.

Chris I'm going to hoover then I'm going to watch TV.

Clair But you haven't even told me what the job is.

He looks back at her for a moment, then goes, leaving her alone. A few more seconds and the piece of music, which has begun in the minor, comes to an end in the major.

IV

Chris is listening to a girl of what? 9 or 10? reciting poems. The girl wears a coat over a nurse's uniform, exactly like Jenny in Scene II.

On stage is a concert grand piano, with the lid closed.

Pause.

Chris (*smiles*) Go on.

Girl
There once was a pianist called Jo
Who played every piece far too slow.
    When she got to the end
    She would turn to a friend
And say: 'You don't have to tell me. I know.'

   Pause.

Chris Go on.

Girl
There once was a girl called Jo Gupta
Who slept with a famous conductor.
    But her friends were naive
    And just wouldn't believe
A famous conductor had fucked her.

   Pause.

Chris Go on.

Girl
There once was a child in a drain
Who longed for the sound of the rain.

But when the storm broke
The poor child awoke
In a stream of unbearable pain.

Slight pause. Chris chuckles. Girl smiles.

Chris Who taught you that?

Girl Mummy did.

Slight pause.

Chris Take off your coat, sweetheart. You look hot. You can't play the piano with your coat on.

Girl I'm not going to play the piano.

Chris Yes you are. You're going to let me hear the piece you're going to play Mummy when she comes home. Take off your coat. Come on.

She unbuttons her coat. He takes it and holds it. Her uniform, though tiny, is not a 'play' uniform but a precise copy of that worn by Jenny.

How are those patients today? How's Charlie?

Girl Charlie's lost a lot of blood.

Chris I hope not.

Girl Now he's on a drip.

Chris I hope it's not all over the playroom carpet, sweetheart, like it was last time. (*Slight pause.*) Why are you wearing a coat anyway?

Girl We were outside.

Chris Oh?

Girl Yes, we were watching a blackbird build its nest.

Chris That's nice.

Girl It sang to us.

Chris That's very nice, only I don't think you were watching a blackbird build its nest. I don't think blackbirds make nests—sweetheart—in October. I think they perch on TV aerials—I think they hop across the grass keeping their legs together and stand suddenly very still, with their heads tipped to the side—but I don't think they make nests.

Girl We saw it. We both saw it. It had moss in its beak.

Chris Then how did it sing? (*Slight pause.*) October is when the leaves change colour, not when birds build their nests—mmm? Aren't you collecting pretty leaves at school? Aren't you getting out nice bright paints and printing leaf-shapes onto sheets of white paper? Eh? (*Smiles.*) Aren't your teachers explaining about the seasons? Haven't they told you how the earth leans away from the sun? (*Slight pause.*) What about conkers? When I was your age my coat pockets were full of them—but yours—well . . .

> *He's still holding her coat. He reaches towards one of the pockets. She makes a tiny move as if to stop him, then checks herself. He notices this, meets her eyes for a moment, smiles, then pushes his hand into the pocket.*

What's this, sweetheart? What's this in your pocket?

> *He withdraws his hand: there's a red sticky substance on his fingers. He lifts his fingers to his nose and sniffs—or perhaps tastes.*

Girl It was Charlie.

Chris What was Charlie?

Girl The blood. It was Charlie.

43

Chris It's no good blaming Charlie. Charlie is too small.

Girl He's not too small to be bad. You should punish him.

Chris He's not bad.

Girl Hit him.

Chris Don't talk like that.

Girl Punish him. Hit him.

Chris Hey hey hey—I said I don't want to hear you talk like that. Understood?

He wipes his fingers on the coat and drops the coat on the ground.

Let me hear your piece, sweetheart.

Girl And he opens doors.

Chris Does what?

Girl He *is* bad. He opens doors. He found Mummy's writing.

Chris You mean her work. Well I hope you've made it tidy.

Girl Not work—writing. She's been writing in a secret diary. He opened her wardrobe and he found a secret diary under her shoes.

Slight pause.

Chris Well I hope you haven't been reading it.

Girl Charlie can't read.

Chris I'm not talking about Charlie. (*Slight pause.*) You do know that it's wrong to read somebody's secret diary. (*Slight pause.*) Think how you'd feel if somebody read your secret diary.

Girl If I had a secret diary no one would ever find it.

Chris But what if they *did* find it? What if they read your secret thoughts.

Girl I don't have any secret thoughts. (*Slight pause.*) I want my coat.

Chris Mmm?

Girl I want my coat back.

Chris Your coat is dirty, sweetheart. Look at it.

Girl I want it back. I'm cold.

Chris You can't be cold. You're indoors. It's October and the heating's on. (*Slight pause.*) Look, if I let you wear your coat, will you play your piece for Mummy when she wakes up?

Girl Mummy's not here. Mummy's at a conference.

Chris Will you?

Girl Mummy's not here.

The girl hesitates, then takes a step towards the coat.

Chris (*stopping her verbally.*) Uh-uh. (*Smiles.*)

He picks up the coat himself and holds it up for her to put on. She comes over, tries to get her arm in the sleeve, but gets in a muddle.

(*Smiles.*) Wrong arm, sweetheart.

They try again and again get in a muddle.

Girl I can't get my arm in.

Chris What's wrong?

Girl I can't get my arm in the right place.

Chris What?—come on—you're / not trying.

Girl I can't get my arm into the sleeve. It's the way you're / holding it.

Chris Alright, alright, just do it yourself. JUST DO THE FUCKING THING YOURSELF.

He moves away, turns his back. The girl calmly puts on the coat and calmly buttons it. Then:

Girl Daddy?

Chris What?

Girl Shall I play you my piece now?

Chris (*begins very soft and fast*) Listen, sweetheart, there's something you ought to know: Mummy came home last night—she came home from Lisbon in the middle of the night—well—like it says in a book— 'unexpectedly'—and went straight to bed. She's here now—yes—that's right—in the house—but I've left her asleep because she was so tired. (*Laughs.*) You should've seen her. She was so worn out that she didn't even go into your room, she didn't even have the strength (she said) to push the hair back behind your ear and kiss you, the way she normally does. Not because she was unhappy—you're not to think that Mummy was unhappy—because—well—in fact she was laughing. That's how I knew she was home. I heard Mummy laughing out in the street—and there she was—under the street-lamp—sharing a joke—something about crocodiles—with the taxi driver out in the street. (*Laughs.*) Oh, it was windy! You should've seen all the leaves swirling round the shiny black taxi under the orange light. And when she came through the front door—still laughing, by the way—guess what: two enormous chestnut leaves followed her right into the house. (*Laughs.*)

46

I said 'Well this is a surprise: I didn't expect you back till the middle of next week!'

Girl And what did Mummy say to that?

Chris Mmm?

Girl And what did Mummy say to that?

Chris I've told you, sweetheart: Mummy was tired—she didn't say anything.

Girl Not even when the leaves came in?

Chris What leaves?

Girl You said two enormous leaves came into the house.

Chris Well yes they did—two enormous leaves *did* come into the house—but Mummy didn't even see them, sweetheart, because of the way she was clinging on to me.

Girl Was she afraid?

Chris (*laughs*) Of course she wasn't afraid. It wasn't that kind of clinging.

Girl Maybe she was afraid that someone would find her secret diary, and that's why she came back home.

Slight pause. In the distance an alarm clock starts ringing.

Chris Why don't you run off and play.

Girl That's Mummy's clock.

Chris I know it's Mummy's clock—and that's why I want you to run off and play.

Girl I want to see her.

Chris You can see her after we've talked.

Girl What are you going to talk about?

Chris We won't know, sweetheart, what we're going to talk about until we start talking. Now off you go.

Girl The diary?

Chris Of course not the diary. The diary—remember?—is a secret. Kiss?

He bends down. She kisses his cheek.

Good girl.

Girl What about the piano?

Chris The piano can wait. Now off you go.

The girl runs off. The alarm clock gets louder and after a few moments Clair appears, holding the clock, which is still ringing. She puts it down on the piano, which makes the sound even louder, and watches it until the ringing stops.

Clair (*turns to him*) Thank you.

Chris Oh?

Clair Thank you—yes—for letting me sleep.

Slight pause.

Chris So how was your conference?

Clair Mmm?

Chris The conference—in Lisbon—how was it?

Clair Oh it was a marvellous conference. People from all over the world converged on Lisbon to talk about books. Can you imagine? Authors read passages from their books and talked about what had inspired them. And the translators talked about the authors and how hard it was to translate the authors and the authors spoke very highly of the translators and were even, some of them, translators themselves, which meant that they had interesting things to say not just about writing but about translating too. And after lunch we'd all go off into little rooms—split up I mean—and go off into little rooms—those funny little rooms they have in Lisbon—take some particular topic—poetry—politics—and really pull it apart—really examine poetry or politics under the knife—put these things really and truly under the knife—just five or six of us in a little room really concentrating—I can't explain what it was like.

Chris You've just told me what it was like.

Clair (*smiles*) No. Because it wasn't like that at all, you see.

  Pause.

And my paper went well.

Chris Good.

Clair Went really well. My hand shook at the beginning, but everybody paid attention—even laughed at my jokes.

Chris You? Jokes?

Clair Yes—because I was nervous—obviously—about the jokes—but the jokes worked.

Chris What jokes? Tell me one.

Clair What?

Chris Tell me a joke.

Clair Not that kind of joke—not a joke you 'tell'—just ways of putting things—phrasing things—and Mohamed was pleased—he came up to me afterwards—in fact he sought me out—

Chris Oh?

49

Clair Yes—sought me out—singled me out I mean in the cafeteria and in front of everyone he knocked me into a table.

Chris Hurt you?

Clair No no—just rushed over to thank me and knocked me backwards into a table. He was so clumsy—this big bear of a man knocking me off my feet—I couldn't help smiling to myself.

Chris Like you are now?

Clair What?

Chris Like you are now—smiling to yourself like you are now?

Clair Of course I'm not smiling to myself. I'm smiling at you.

Chris Oh? Are you? Why?

Clair Of course I'm smiling at you. You're my husband. You're my husband, and— What're you doing?

Chris Sorry?

Clair You backed away.

Chris I did what?

Clair You backed away.

Chris No.

Clair I stepped towards you and you backed away. You know you did. (*Slight pause.*) Why did you back away from me?

    Pause.

Look. I'm here. I'm home. What more do you want from me? Try to understand. I open my door and what do I see? A man I very much respect. He wants to talk. He says he has a confession to make. What d'you mean, Mohamed, I say, a confession, can't it wait. No, it can't wait, he has to talk to me now, right now. Alright, Mohamed, let's go downstairs, I say, let's go down to the bar together, let's talk there. I can't, says Mohamed, I can't say what I have to say to you in the bar. So—look—I'm not stupid—I tell Mohamed that in that case he'll have to wait till morning because it's late, I'm tired, and I want to go to bed. No, says Mohamed, I have to come in, you have to let me talk, there's something I need to confess, don't close the door. So what can I do? D'you see? Mmm? Try to understand. Because this is a man that I very much respect—because of what he's suffered—and written about. So I let him into my room and he sits down in front of the window which I've kept open because of the heat and he says to me my child is dead. I say what d'you mean Mohamed, your child is dead? He says she's been knocked over by a car, she's dead, I just had a call from my sister-in-law. You mean the little girl I saw at the station? Yes, he says—Laela—she was crossing the road to post a letter. And he just sits there in front of the window looking down at his hands.

Slight pause.

Chris Waiting for you to comfort him.

Clair What?

Chris He was waiting for you to / comfort him.

Clair Well obviously—yes—I thought—of course I did—thought about going to him—putting my arm around him—thought about attempting to comfort him. But that's when he looked up at me. He looked up at me and what was strange was that his eyes—which were grey—had always been grey—were grey at the station—were grey in the cafeteria—his eyes had turned—and I don't mean the light—I mean the eyes themselves—had turned black. His eyes had turned black like the inside of a poppy and he said to me, I still haven't confessed. I said, look Mohamed, you're upset, you don't need to confess, you need to go to your sister-in-law, you need to try and sleep, let's see if there's a pharmacy still open. He said to me, no no no I still haven't confessed. And this time he frightened me.

Chris You should've asked him to leave.

Clair Of course, but how? I said, you've got nothing to confess, Mohamed, it was an accident. Oh yes, he said, it was an accident, but listen Clair, what you have to know, and what I didn't tell you when we first met, is why I sent my little girl away. I sent her away because she got under my feet, because she stopped me writing, because she constantly interrupted my work, and sometimes, when I shouted at her, because she had interrupted my work, to ask for a drink, or to be read a story, her small body jerked back, he said, as if hit by a bullet. Me, he said, a writer, refusing my own child a story. Come on, Mohamed, I said, come on, we all get angry with our children, it's normal. No, said Mohamed, nothing a writer does is normal, and besides that's not what I'm confessing, because that is, as you say, something that is entirely human and banal. No, what I have to tell you is that the moment I finished speaking to my sister-in-law tonight, and put down the phone, I experienced—and the nearest thing to the word he used is 'exaltation'—I experienced a secret exaltation, he said, as I realised that what had happened could only enhance my work. My child, you see, is like a log thrown into the fire, making the fire burn, he said, more brightly.

Pause.

Chris Thrown into the fire.

Clair That's what he said—yes—like a piece of wood. So I was very angry then—with Mohamed. I told him I didn't care how many people he'd killed in his never-ending fight for freedom and democracy, or how many days he'd been tortured or how many prizes he'd won for describing it. I told him I was disgusted by what he called his exhilaration or his exaltation or whatever the fuck it was and I wanted him out—I wanted him to GET OUT OF MY ROOM.

Chris And did he?

Clair I'm sorry?

Chris Did he get out of your room?

Pause. She looks away.

So you believed him.

Clair Yes. No. Of course I did. Believed what?

Chris That his child was dead.

Clair Laela. Yes. He told me.

Chris So she won't be needing the diary then.

Pause. She meets his eyes. He smiles at her.

V

Jenny alone, wearing pink jeans and high-heeled shoes. She takes out a mirror and inspects her face. She puts away the mirror. She looks at the piano, whose lid is now up. She runs her fingers over the keyboard without making any sound.

Clair enters.

Jenny It's very nice here. I had no idea—to be honest— it would be so nice inside your house. It's warm—and surprisingly peaceful. You have such lovely things, like this piano. And I've just realised that now the leaves have gone, I can see my own windows. (*Slight pause.*) Oh—and this is for you.

> *She hands Clair a small parcel, which Clair begins to unwrap.*

Clair You're right. It's a nice house. It's warm in every sense. We're very happy here.

> *Pause.*

Jenny How're your children?

Clair Mmm?

Jenny How're your children?

Clair They're not bothering you, are they?

Jenny What?

Clair I said: they're not bothering you—not keeping you awake.

Jenny Oh no. I don't hear them. Or if I do it makes me feel . . . well . . . Hmm.

Clair finishes unwrapping the present: a small serrated kitchen knife.

(*Smiles.*) I hope you like it. I thought it would be useful with small children.

Clair Oh?

Jenny To cut up their food.

Clair You're right. (*Goes to kiss her.*) Thank you.

Jenny Careful! (*Steps back.*)

Clair Mmm?

Jenny The knife.

Clair Of course. Sorry. (*Points the knife away or puts it down.*) Thank you, Jenny. (*Kisses her.*)

Slight pause.

Jenny I haven't seen your children.

Clair Oh they're probably racing up and down excitedly on their new bikes.

Jenny What, with your husband?

Clair Mmm?

Jenny With your husband?

Clair Oh no—my husband found a job—he's working.

Jenny What? At Christmas?

Clair You sound surprised, but surely it's not unusual. It's not just doctors and soldiers, it's not just nurses like yourself, Jenny, who work at Christmas-time. Commerce can't stop any more than the course—isn't this right?—

of some fatal diseases. And while you and I are sitting in front of the fire like this,* unwrapping our gifts, people still need to buy things.

Pause.

What's wrong?

Jenny I don't know. Nothing feels right. Everything—don't you think?—seems awkward and artificial. I put these shoes on specially—but I'm not really comfortable in them—and if I'm honest, I don't know why I'm wearing them. Even a normal conversation like this—with a person I like—because I certainly like you—don't get me wrong—but even this—I don't know why—seems strained. I don't really know why I'm here at all.

Clair (*smiles*) You're here, Jenny, because I invited you. And if your shoes feel uncomfortable—well—simple—take them off.

Jenny You say your children are out on their bikes—but I can't hear them—I didn't see one single child when I walked here from my flat—nobody was out—it was so quiet—it was unnatural.

Clair Christmas is always like that: everyone's indoors with their families.

Jenny It didn't feel right. There were no smells in the air. People had wreaths on their front doors, but I couldn't see anybody through the windows, even though they had lights flashing round the window frames. And before I came out, I spoke to my husband and he just sounded angry.

Clair Maybe he misses you.

* *There is no fire. They are not sitting.*

Jenny Well that's not my fault.

Christopher enters. He wears the outfit of a supermarket butcher's assistant: a white hat with a brim, a white smock, and pinned to the smock a badge with his name: 'Chris'.

Chris (*kisses Clair on the cheek*) Hello sweetheart. We have a guest.

Clair This is Jenny.

Chris Jenny. Of course. Hello.

Clair How was work?

Chris Totally mad. Sam's off sick and Janine can't tell a pig's ear from a cow's arsehole, scuse my French. (*Chuckles.*) But listen: we know each other.

Jenny Yes.

Chris Don't we.

Jenny Yes.

Chris Wednesdays.

Jenny That's right.

Chris Wednesday afternoons: minced steak—two hundred grams.

Jenny Yes.

Chris I find myself asking: who is it who's eating those two hundred grams of minced steak.

Jenny I am.

Chris Not the dog then.

Jenny I'm sorry?

Chris Because 9 times out of 10 it's the dog. Guaranteed.

Slight pause.

Clair You should take off your hat.

Chris Mmm?

Clair Take off your hat. And don't wear your badge indoors. We know who you are.

Chris I'm Christopher. (*Grins.*)

Clair Exactly. You're my husband.

Chris I'm Christopher. I'm her husband. And I want my present. I don't want to take off my hat. I like my hat. I want my present.

Clair What makes you think I've got you a present?

Chris Well if she hasn't got me a present I'll break her fucking neck. (*Chuckles.*) Translate *that* into English—eh?

Clair I'll go and get it.

She goes. Pause.

Chris How's the war?

Jenny Mmm?

Chris The war. How's the war?

Jenny Oh, the war's fine, thank you.

Chris Going well?

Jenny Mmm?

Chris Going well, is it?

Jenny I think so.

Slight pause.

Chris And the enemy? How's the enemy?

Jenny Intractable.

Chris Oh?

Jenny Pretty intractable, yes.

Chris Bastards.

Slight pause.

Are you comfortable in those shoes?

Jenny What? Yes, I'm fine.

Chris Because if you're not comfortable / take them off.

Jenny I'm absolutely fine. Thank you.

Clair enters with gift.

Clair What is it?

Jenny Nothing.

Clair Is something wrong?

Jenny Of course not—no—we were chatting.

Chris What's this then?

Jenny Just chatting away.

Chris I said what's this?

Clair Open it.

He takes the present, opens it. It's the diary from Scene I.

Chris It's a diary.

Clair Yes.

Chris But it's been written in.

Clair Yes.

Chris Why's it been written in?

He flicks through the diary, stops at a page, reads softly.

'. . . a different person . . . to the person who is writing this now . . .' Hmm.

He flicks through, reads softly.

'. . . then I myself—this is what I imagined—could come . . .' (*Peers at word.*) What's this word?

Clair Alive—come alive.

Chris '. . . I myself—this is what I imagined—could come alive.' Hmm.

Pause. He looks at her.

Clair Go on.

Chris Go on what?

Jenny She means read it—don't you.

Clair Yes. Read it.

Chris reads softly, finding the words not always easy to decipher, following them with his finger. He's not a 'good' reader. He seems generally oblivious to the sense of what he's reading.

Chris 'When I was young—much younger than now—a different person you might even say—to the person who is writing this now—and before I began to make my living from translation—taking refuge in it as one writer says "the way an alcoholic takes refuge in alcoholism"—before that I truly believed there was . . .' (*Peers at word.*) Can't read it.

Clair A city.

Chris A what?

Clair A city.

Chris '. . . truly believed there was'—that's right—'a city inside of me—a huge and varied city full of green squares, shops and churches, secret streets, and hidden doors leading to staircases that climbed to rooms full of light where there would be drops of rain on the windows, and where in each small drop the whole city would be seen, upside down. There would be industrial zones where elevated trains ran past the windows of factories and conference centres. There would be schools where, when there was a lull in the traffic, you could hear children playing. The seasons in the city would be distinct: hot summer nights when everyone slept with their windows open, or sat out on their balconies in their underwear, drinking beer from the fridge—and in winter, very cold mornings when snow had settled in courtyards and they showed the snow on TV and the snow on TV was the same snow out in the street, shovelled to the side to enable the inhabitants to get to work. And I was convinced that in this city of mine I would find an inex . . .' (*Peers at word.*)

Clair Inexhaustible.

Chris '. . . an inexhaustible source of characters and stories for my writing. I was convinced that in order to be a writer I'd simply have to travel to this city—the one inside of me—and write down what I discovered there.'

Slight pause.

Clair Go on.

Chris 'I knew it would be difficult to reach this city. It wouldn't be like going on a plane to Marrakech, say, or Lisbon. I knew the journey could take days or even years quite possibly. But I knew that if I could find life in my city, and be able to describe life, the stories and characters of life, then I myself—this is what I imagined—could come alive. And I did reach my city. Yes. Oh yes. But when I reached it found it had been destroyed. The houses had been destroyed, and so had the shops. Minarets lay on the ground next to church steeples. What . . . balconies'? (*Momentarily confused.*) 'What balconies there were had dropped to the pavement. There were no children in the playgrounds, only coloured lines. I looked for inhabitants to write about, but there were no inhabitants, just dust. I looked for the people still clinging on to life—what stories they could tell!—but even there—in the drains, the basements—in the underground railway system—there was nothing—nobody—just dust. And this grey dust, like the ash from a cigarette, was so fine it got into my pen and stopped the ink reaching the page. Could this really be all that was inside of me? I cried at first but then I pulled myself together and tried for a while then to invent. I invented . . .' (*Peers at word.*) What?

Clair Characters.

Chris '. . . characters . . . invented characters . . .' (*Loses his place, finds it again.*) 'I invented characters and I put them in my city. The one I called Mohamed. The one I called the nurse—Jenny—she was funny. I invented a child too, I was quite pleased with the child. But it was a struggle. They wouldn't come alive. They lived a little—but only the way a sick bird tortured by a cat lives in a shoebox. It was hard to make them speak normally—and their stories fell apart even as I was telling them. Sometimes I even . . .' (*Peers at word.*) What's this?

Clair Dressed them up.

Chris Mmm?

Clair Dressed them—dressed / them up.

Chris 'Sometimes I even'—okay—'dressed them up the way I used to dress my dolls when I was little. I put them in funny clothes but then I felt ashamed. And when they looked at me, they looked at me—like it says in a book—"accusingly".'

The little girl appears, dressed exactly like Jenny: pink jeans, high-heeled shoes. She sits at the piano.

'So I gave up on my city. I was no writer—that much was clear. I'd like to say how sad the discovery of my own emptiness made me, but the truth is I feel as I write this down nothing but relief.'

He turns the pages looking for more text, but finds none. He closes the diary and looks at Clair.

What about me?

Clair What about you?

Chris Am I / invented too?

Clair Why don't you take off your hat now? What?

Chris Me. Am I invented too?

Clair No more than I am, surely. Take off your hat.

Jenny Yes. Go on. Take it off.

Chris Why?

Clair Because it will be better.

He slowly removes his hat.

You see: much better.

Chris You think?

Clair Much better. (*To Jenny.*) Don't you agree?

Jenny Oh yes. Yes. Much better like that.

Clair (*to Girl*) Play us your piece, sweetheart.

Jenny Much much better like that.

The Girl begins to play the Schubert movement heard in Scene III. She sets off confidently but gets stuck at bar 3. She starts again but is soon in difficulty. The light begins to fade. She can't get beyond bar 4.